PICTURE THIS
ANIMALS

 KINGFISHER

First published 2014 by Kingfisher
an imprint of Macmillan Children's Books
a division of Macmillan Publishers Limited
20 New Wharf Road, London N1 9RR
Basingstoke and Oxford
Associated companies throughout the world
www.panmacmillan.com

Author: Margaret Hynes
Illustrations: Andy Crisp
Consultant: John Woodward
Designer: Samantha Richiardi
Developed by: Simon Holland

With special thanks to Peter Winfield

ISBN 978-0-7534-3502-1

1 3 5 7 9 8 6 4 2
1TR/0913/WKT/UG/140WF

A CIP catalogue record for this book
is available from the British Library.

Printed in China

PICTURE THIS
ANIMALS

picnic area 30km

KINGFISHER

Contents

6 Metric measures

8 Animal kingdom

10 Mammals

12 Mammal lifestyles

14 Bird abilities

16 Reptile groups

18 Amphibians

20 Fish features

22 Swimming styles

24 Deep-sea life

26 Spineless creatures

28 Ingenious invertebrates

30 Minute creatures

32 Animal champions

34 Animal senses

36 Communication

38 Hunters

40 Animal defences

42 Criminals

44 Courtship

46 Growing up

48 Life expectancy

50 Animal homes

52 Migrating animals

54 Adaptations

56 Conservation

58 Useful charts

60 Glossary

62 Index

64 Find out more

Metric measures

This book is bursting with information graphics, or pictures, that illustrate facts and figures relating to animals. Any measurements are shown using the metric system, which describes length in metres, volume in litres and weight in kilograms. If you use feet, pints and pounds instead, you are using the imperial system. The graphics on these pages compare metric and imperial amounts, and will help you to visualize the metric units.

Speed

Km/h is a unit of speed, expressing the number of kilometres travelled in one hour. This speedometer shows how km/h compare with miles per hour (mph).

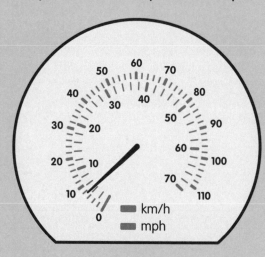

Volume

There are 1,000 millilitres in one litre. This is about 35 fluid ounces (35 fl oz) or just over two US pints.

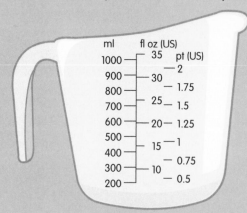

Distance

HIGHWAY 50

Newtown 1km (0.6 miles)

Townsville 10km (6 miles)

Length

There are ten millimetres (10mm) in one centimetre (1cm), 100 centimetres in one metre (1m) and 1,000 metres in one kilometre (1km). This ruler shows centimetres (cm) and inches (in).

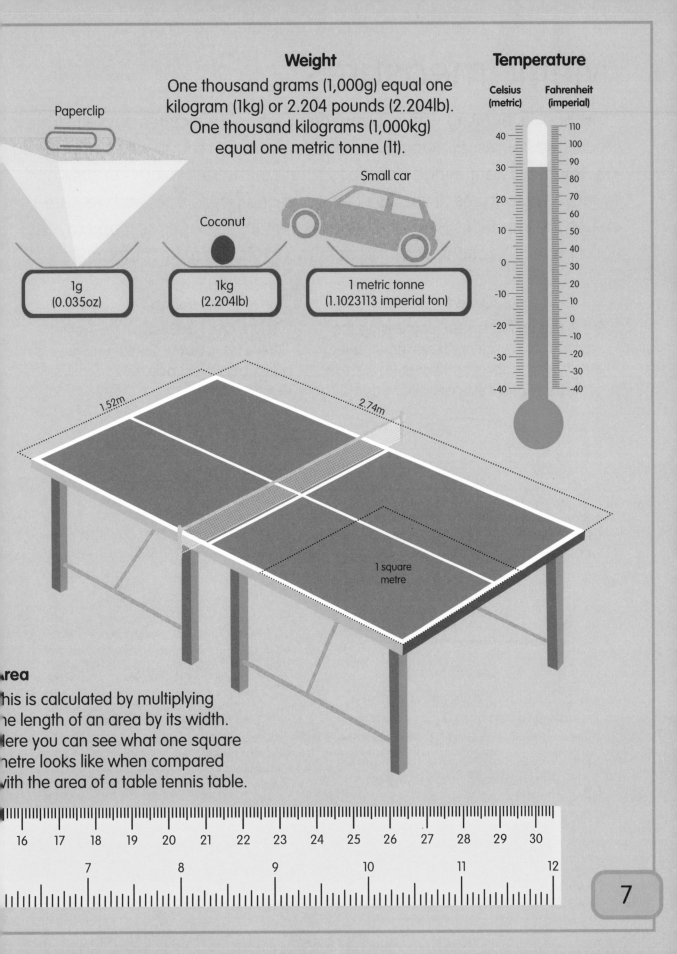

Weight

One thousand grams (1,000g) equal one kilogram (1kg) or 2.204 pounds (2.204lb). One thousand kilograms (1,000kg) equal one metric tonne (1t).

Paperclip

Coconut

Small car

1g
(0.035oz)

1kg
(2.204lb)

1 metric tonne
(1.1023113 imperial ton)

Temperature

Celsius
(metric)

Fahrenheit
(imperial)

1.52m

2.74m

1 square
metre

Area

This is calculated by multiplying the length of an area by its width. Here you can see what one square metre looks like when compared with the area of a table tennis table.

Animal kingdom

When a new animal species is found, it is given a scientific name, usually in Latin, and a formal description that explains how the species differs from other species, or how it is related to them. The species is classified, or arranged, into categories based on shared features. All animals belong to the animal kingdom, and all dog-like animals are grouped in the dog family.

Animal catalogues

Category	Number of groups in the category
Animal Kingdom	1
Phylum	32
Class	90
Order	493
Family	5,404
Genus	94,240
Species	1,233,500

Classifying *Canis lupus* (grey wolf)

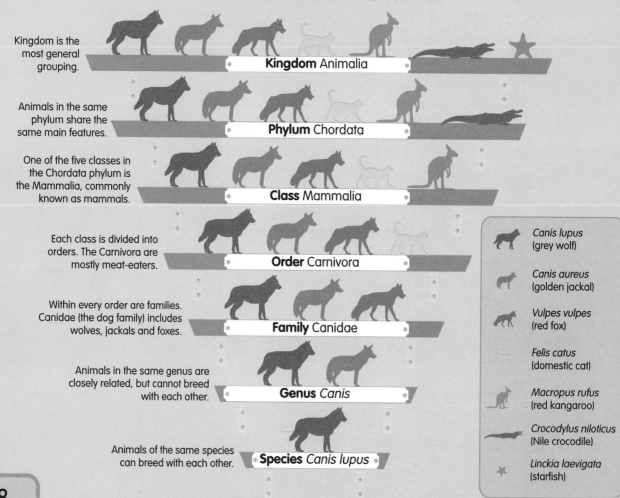

Kingdom Animalia

Kingdom is the most general grouping.

Phylum Chordata

Animals in the same phylum share the same main features.

Class Mammalia

One of the five classes in the Chordata phylum is the Mammalia, commonly known as mammals.

Order Carnivora

Each class is divided into orders. The Carnivora are mostly meat-eaters.

Family Canidae

Within every order are families. Canidae (the dog family) includes wolves, jackals and foxes.

Genus *Canis*

Animals in the same genus are closely related, but cannot breed with each other.

Species *Canis lupus*

Animals of the same species can breed with each other.

Canis lupus (grey wolf)

Canis aureus (golden jackal)

Vulpes vulpes (red fox)

Felis catus (domestic cat)

Macropus rufus (red kangaroo)

Crocodylus niloticus (Nile crocodile)

Linckia laevigata (starfish)

Identified and described

86% are yet to be described

14% are catalogued

Out of this 14%...

...95% are invertebrates (with no backbone)

...15% are vertebrates

Out of this 15%...

...48% are fish

...19% are birds

...15% are reptiles

...9% are amphibians

...9% are mammals

Land animal descriptions

12%

88% are yet to be identified and described

Ocean animal descriptions

8%

92% are yet to be identified and described

9

Mammals

All mammals are warm-blooded creatures that keep their bodies at a constant temperature by generating their own heat. Mammals also have some fur or hair on their bodies, and feed their young milk. A few mammals lay eggs, but most mammals give birth to live young. Some of these mammals carry their young in pouches.

Top six mammal groups

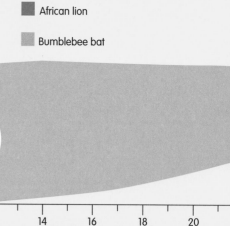

Mammal orders (6 of 27)		Number of species
	Rodentia (mice, rats, porcupines, beavers and other gnawing animals)	2,225
	Chiroptera (bats)	1,150
	Eulipotyphla (shrews, moles and solenodons)	607
	Primates (humans, apes, monkeys and lemurs)	414
	Cetartiodactyla (whales and even-toed hoofed mammals)	330
	Carnivora (Dogs, cats, bears, weasels, seals and their relatives)	285
Known species in the top six orders		**5,011**
Total number of known mammal species		**5,488**

From Australia and New Guinea

Egg-laying mammals

An echidna usually lays one egg. A platypus lays about three.

From Australia

Different shapes and sizes

Mammals range in size from the 40mm-long bumblebee bat to the 33m-long blue whale.

■ Blue whale   ■ Human   ■ African lion

■ African elephant   ■ Kangaroo   ■ Bumblebee bat

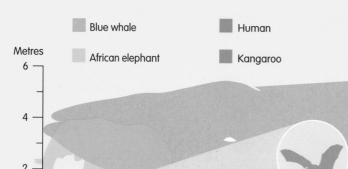

Metres

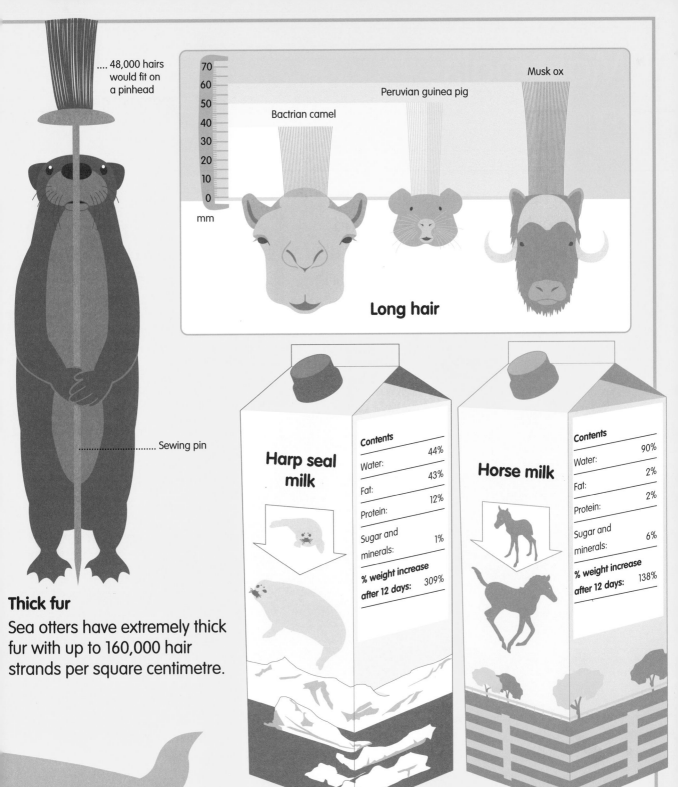

.... 48,000 hairs would fit on a pinhead

Bactrian camel

Peruvian guinea pig

Musk ox

70
60
50
40
30
20
10
0
mm

Long hair

.... Sewing pin

Thick fur
Sea otters have extremely thick fur with up to 160,000 hair strands per square centimetre.

Harp seal milk

Contents	
Water:	44%
Fat:	43%
Protein:	12%
Sugar and minerals:	1%
% weight increase after 12 days:	309%

Horse milk

Contents	
Water:	90%
Fat:	2%
Protein:	2%
Sugar and minerals:	6%
% weight increase after 12 days:	138%

Mother's milk
The more protein there is in an animal's milk the faster its young gain weight by drinking it.

Metres

26   28   30   32   34

Mammal lifestyles

In general, small, very active mammals tend to eat a lot of food in relation to their size to fuel their activity, and they produce a lot of waste. Large, less active mammals that graze all day don't need very much sleep. Some mammals hibernate, going into a dormant (inactive) state for long periods of time in the winter when food is scarce.

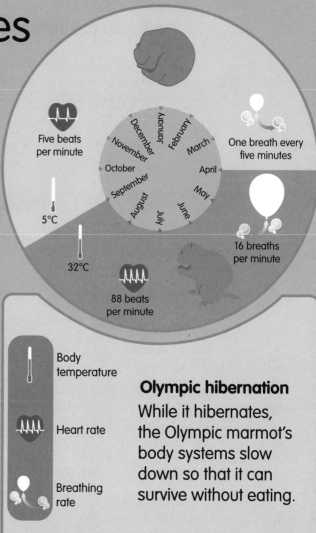

Five beats per minute

One breath every five minutes

5°C

32°C

16 breaths per minute

88 beats per minute

Body temperature

Heart rate

Breathing rate

Olympic hibernation

While it hibernates, the Olympic marmot's body systems slow down so that it can survive without eating.

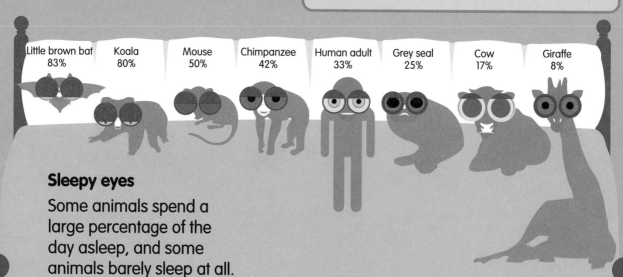

| Little brown bat 83% | Koala 80% | Mouse 50% | Chimpanzee 42% | Human adult 33% | Grey seal 25% | Cow 17% | Giraffe 8% |

Sleepy eyes

Some animals spend a large percentage of the day asleep, and some animals barely sleep at all.

Daily food consumption and waste production

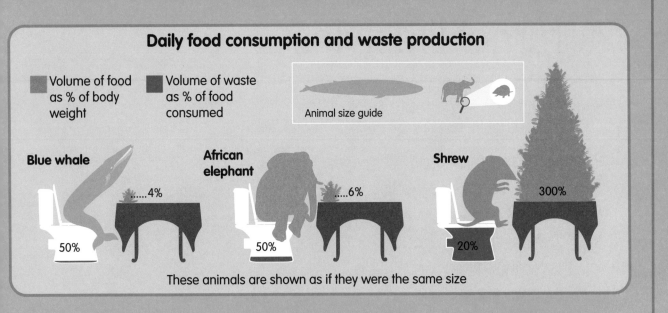

■ Volume of food as % of body weight
■ Volume of waste as % of food consumed

Animal size guide

Blue whale 4% 50%

African elephant 6% 50%

Shrew 300% 20%

These animals are shown as if they were the same size

Gas power
Some animals release enough waste gas to power a 100-watt light bulb.

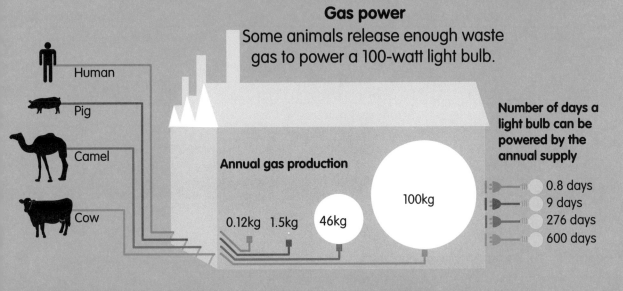

Human
Pig
Camel
Cow

Annual gas production

0.12kg 1.5kg 46kg 100kg

Number of days a light bulb can be powered by the annual supply

0.8 days
9 days
276 days
600 days

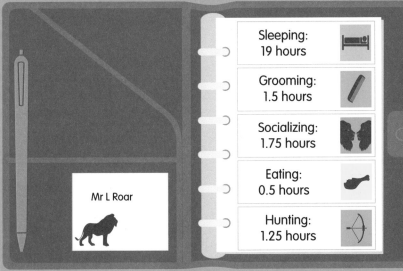

Mr L Roar

Sleeping: 19 hours

Grooming: 1.5 hours

Socializing: 1.75 hours

Eating: 0.5 hours

Hunting: 1.25 hours

A lion's daily routine
Lions work extremely hard in short bursts of activity to catch the food they need. But, they get to spend the rest of the day relaxing.

Bird abilities

Birds are probably best known for their ability to fly. But not all birds are flying aces. Certain species, such as ostriches and penguins, can't fly and have lifestyles that are more suited to the land or water. All birds have feathers and reproduce by laying eggs. These vary in shape, colour and size, depending on the type of bird that lays them.

High fliers

The maximum recorded flying heights for certain birds.

12,000m

Rüppell's griffon vulture
11,300m

Jet aircraft
10,700m

10,000m

Bar-headed goose
9,000m

Whooper swan
8,840m

Mount Everest
8,848m

8,000m

6,000m

Mallard
6,400m

Denali (Mount McKinley)
6,194m

White stork
4,800m

4,000m

Lapwing
3,900m

Fieldfare
3,300m

Light aircraft
3,000m

2,000m

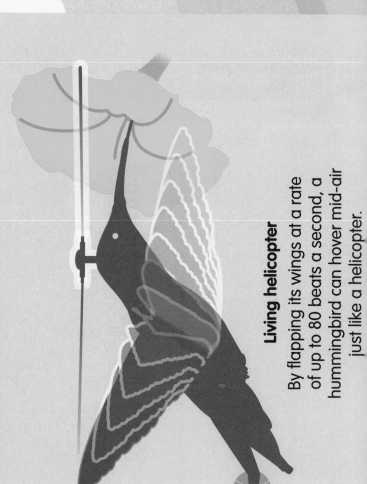

Living helicopter

By flapping its wings at a rate of up to 80 beats a second, a hummingbird can hover mid-air just like a helicopter.

Deep divers

Some birds plunge into water from the air, or from the water's surface, to catch fish. Penguins chase fish by propelling themselves through the water using their wings.

Sea level (0m)

-100m

-200m

-300m

-400m

-500m

-600m

Peruvian diving petrel
-83m

Thick-billed murre
-210m

Record-breaking divers
using special equipment
-330m

Emperor penguin
-540m

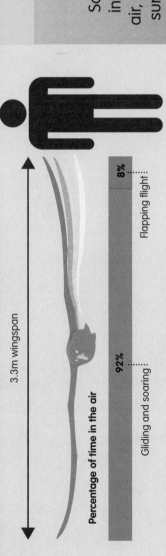

3.3m wingspan

Percentage of time in the air

92%

8%

Gliding and soaring

Flapping flight

Giant glider

The wandering albatross can spend several hours gliding and soaring through the air without flapping its giant wings once.

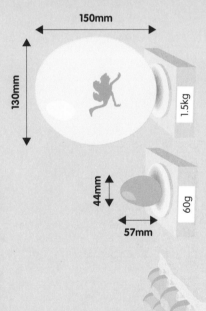

150mm

130mm

1.5kg

44mm

57mm

60g

Extraordinary egg

The largest living bird, the ostrich, lays the largest of all birds' eggs – they are about 24 times the size of a chicken's egg.

15

Reptile groups

All reptiles have scaly skin and bony skeletons with backbones. Most of these creatures lay eggs, but a few give birth to live young. Reptiles are cold-blooded creatures that rely on their surroundings for warmth. They must adjust their activities and behaviour to suit the changing temperature of their environment.

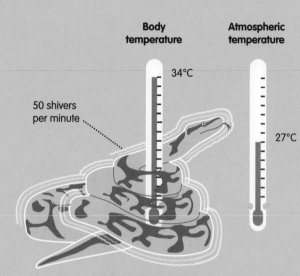

Body temperature

Atmospheric temperature

34°C

50 shivers per minute

27°C

Shivering snake

To keep her eggs warm, a brooding Australian diamond python coils around them, then shivers to raise her body temperature by up to 7°C above the temperature around her.

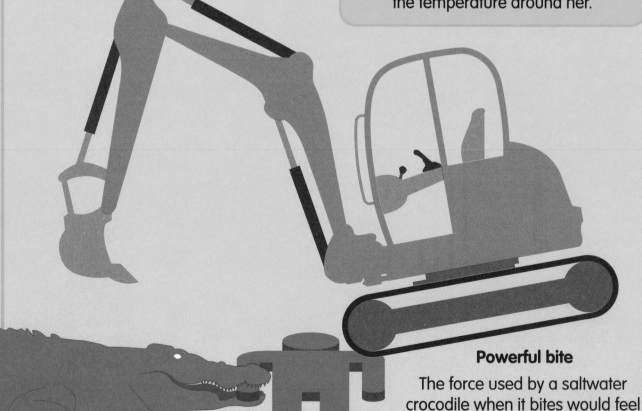

1.7 metric tonnes of force

Powerful bite

The force used by a saltwater crocodile when it bites would feel like the weight of a mini-digger is crushing the area being bitten.

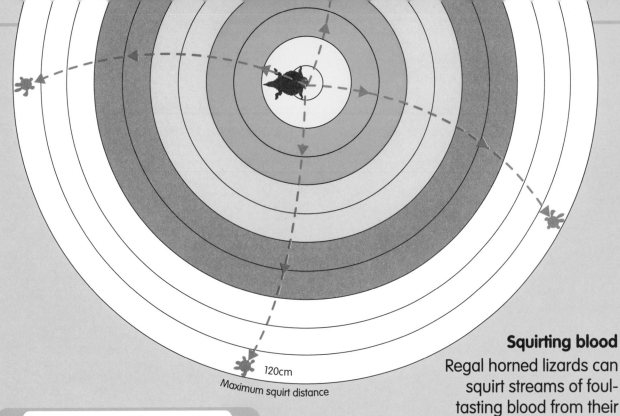

120cm
Maximum squirt distance

Squirting blood

Regal horned lizards can squirt streams of foul-tasting blood from their eyes to repel attackers.

Reptiles

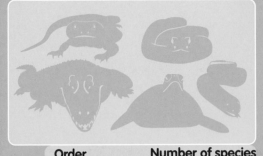

Order	Number of species
Serpentines (snakes)	3,378
Crocodilia (crocodiles, alligators, caimans and gharials)	25
Testudines (turtles, terrapins and tortoises)	327
Sauria (lizards)	5,634
Rhynchocephalia (tuataras)	2
Amphisbaenia (worm lizards)	181
Total number of known species	9,547

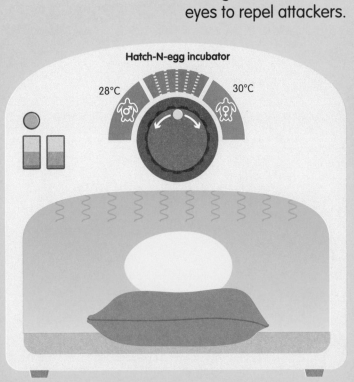

Hatch-N-egg incubator

28°C   30°C

Boy or girl?

Turn the dial to 28°C and a male loggerhead turtle will hatch out of the egg. About 30°C will produce a female turtle instead.

17

Amphibians

Most amphibians start life in the water, but later change physically so they can live on the land, then return to the water to mate. Amphibians are cold-blooded animals, so, like reptiles, an amphibian's body temperature changes with the changing temperature of its surroundings. These creatures breathe through their skin as well as their lungs.

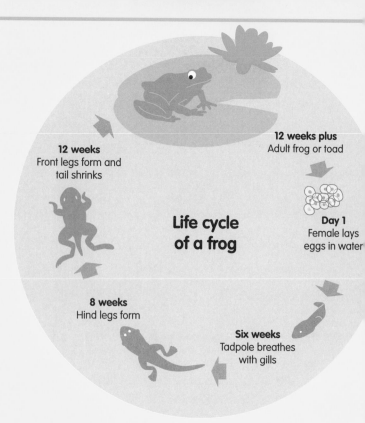

Life cycle of a frog

12 weeks plus
Adult frog or toad

Day 1
Female lays eggs in water

Six weeks
Tadpole breathes with gills

8 weeks
Hind legs form

12 weeks
Front legs form and tail shrinks

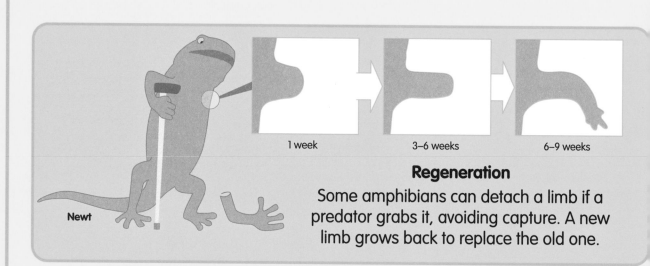

1 week

3–6 weeks

6–9 weeks

Newt

Regeneration

Some amphibians can detach a limb if a predator grabs it, avoiding capture. A new limb grows back to replace the old one.

Leap frog

The mascarene frog can leap to a distance of about 110 times its own length.

0m   1m   2m

Amphibians

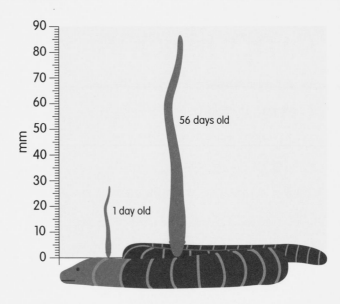

Amphibian orders	Number of species
Anura (frogs and toads)	5,966
Caudata (salamanders and newts)	619
Gymnphiona (caecilians)	186
Total number of known amphibian species	6,771

90
80
70
60 56 days old
50
mm **40**
30
20 1 day old
10
0

Yummy mummy
Taita Hills caecilian hatchlings grow big by feeding on their mother's nutrient-rich skin.

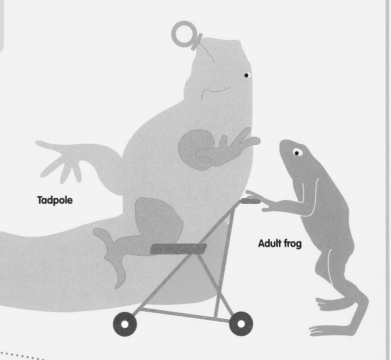

Big baby
Paradoxical frog tadpoles are about four times larger than their parents.

Tadpole

Adult frog

The frogs in this row are shown in scale with the rule measuring the distance of the leap.

3m   4m   5m   5.25m

Fish features

Most species of fish have scales all over their body, fins, a tail, and they are generally streamlined in shape. Fish lay eggs or give birth to live young, and breathe by absorbing oxygen in the water using their gills. There are three main groups of fish: bony fish, jawless fish and cartilaginous fish. Instead of bone, a cartilaginous fish's skeleton is made of flexible tissue called cartilage.

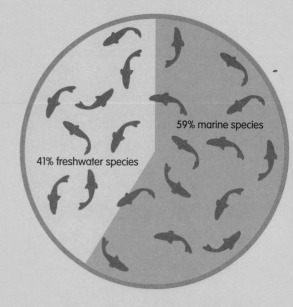

Marine vs freshwater fish
There are more fish species in the sea than are found in freshwater lakes, rivers and ponds.

59% marine species

41% freshwater species

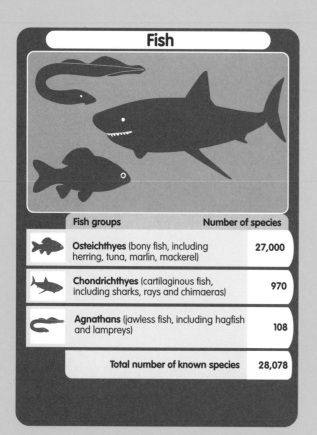

Fish

Fish groups	Number of species
Osteichthyes (bony fish, including herring, tuna, marlin, mackerel)	27,000
Chondrichthyes (cartilaginous fish, including sharks, rays and chimaeras)	970
Agnathans (jawless fish, including hagfish and lampreys)	108
Total number of known species	28,078

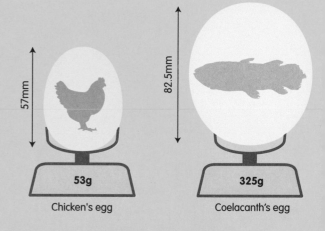

57mm

82.5mm

53g
Chicken's egg

325g
Coelacanth's egg

Heaviest fish egg
The eggs of a coelacanth fish are unusually large for fish eggs – they weigh almost seven times that of a chicken's egg.

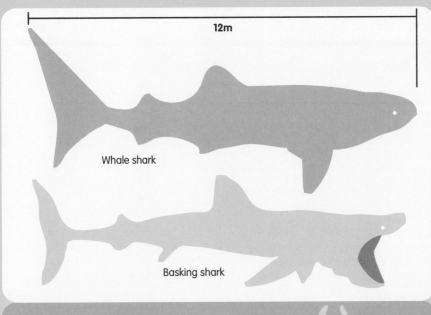

12m

Whale shark

Basking shark

Great white shark

Manta ray

Greater spotted dogfish

Ratfish

Thornback ray

17cm

Dwarf lanternshark

Boneless fish

Cartilaginous fish, which include sharks, skates and rays, come in a variety of shapes and sizes.

Showing their age

As a fish grows and gets older, rings form around the centre of each scale. The rings formed in winter are closer together than those that form in the summer.

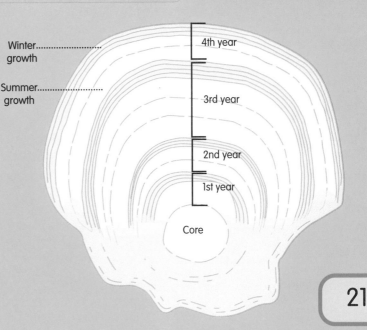

Winter growth

Summer growth

4th year

3rd year

2nd year

1st year

Core

21

Wavy motion of parts of the body	Anguilliform	Subcarangiform
Side view of swimming fish	Eel	Trout
Overhead view of swimming movement		

Wavy motion of certain fins	Rajiform	Diodontiform
Side view of swimming fish	Skate	Balloonfish

Swimming styles

Some fish move through the water by contracting bands of muscles in sequence on alternate sides of their body. This causes their body and tail to move in S-shaped waves. Other fish use their fins to give them thrust in the water, either by moving the fins in a wavy motion or by flapping them.

Key
Parts of the fish that move to provide thrust in the water

Types of fish fins
Caudal
Dorsal
Pectoral
Anal
Pelvic

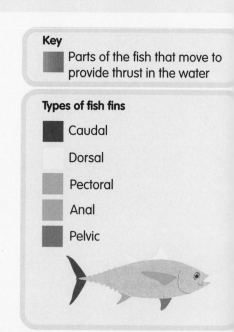

Carangiform

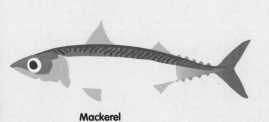

Mackerel

Thunniform

Tuna

Amiiform

Bowfin

Gymnotiform

Banded knifefish

Balistiform

Picasso triggerfish

Flapping motion of certain fins

Side view of swimming fish

Labriform

California sheephead

Tetraodontiform

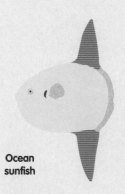

Ocean sunfish

23

Deep-sea life

Scientists divide the oceans into layers, including the twilight zone and dark zone. There is just enough light in the twilight zone for animals to hunt by. The creatures here tend to have large eyes to cope with the dim light. Many of the animals living in the darkness below 1,000m have gaping mouths to make the most of what little food falls down from above. Some of the animals here produce bioluminescent light to lure prey or confuse predators.

200m

TWILIGHT ZONE

1,000m

DARK ZONE

2,000m

3,000m

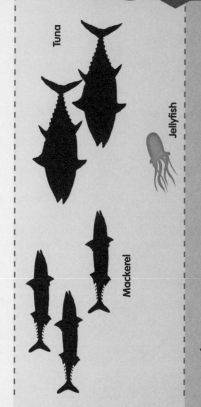

Tuna

Jellyfish

Mackerel

Shark

Squid

Comb jelly

Giant
hatchetfish

Crinoid

Deep-sea

Distribution of ocean animals

Day		Night	
10% above 200m		40% above 200m	
75% twilight zone		50% twilight zone	
15% dark zone		10% dark zone	

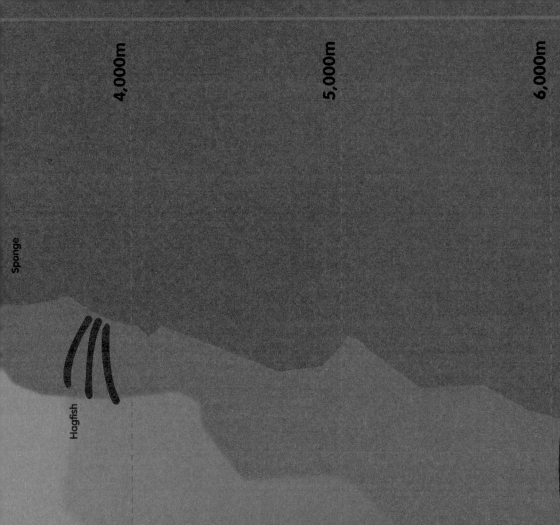

4,000m

5,000m

6,000m

Sponge

Hagfish

Black swallower

Cusk eel

25

Spineless creatures

About 95 per cent of all animal species are invertebrates – animals that don't have a backbone. This group includes worms, slugs, snails and squid, as well as arthropods such as insects, arachnids and crustaceans. Many invertebrates have outer skeletons, which are moulted (shed) by the animals as they grow.

Arthropods and others
There are four times as many species of arthropods as there are other invertebrate species.

World's longest animal
To give you a picture of the giant ribbon worm's 30m-length, the creature is shown here draped on the Statue of Liberty.

Mirror image
Most invertebrates have a symmetrical body – one half of the body looks exactly the same as the other half.

Which dressing-up box belongs to an insect and which one belongs to an arachnid?

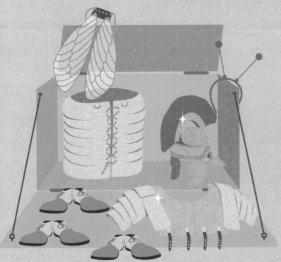

Clues

1) Arachnids usually have eight legs and eight feet. 2) Insects have a head and two body parts.
3) Insects usually have wings. 4) Arachnids usually have eight eyes. 5) Insects usually have antennae.

Moult A   **Moult B**

Outgrowing outerwear

During the few hours after moulting, a tarantula's body grows by up to 50 per cent.

Ingenious invertebrates

Meat-eating invertebrates have specialized tools and skills to help them capture and eat prey. Some invertebrates, such as hookworms, are parasites that actually invade the body of their victim so that they can feed on the nutrient-rich blood inside.

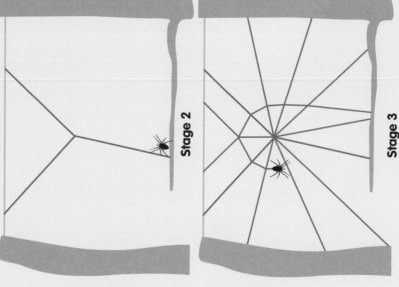

Stage 1

Stage 2

Stage 3

Power and strength

The claws of the plant- and meat-eating coconut crab can cut through a broom handle and are strong enough to lift an average-sized 8-year-old boy.

Weight: 30kg

Blood sucker

In its five-year lifetime, the 12mm-long New World hookworm consumes almost a litre of its human host's blood.

Human blood

The New World hookworm and litre bottle are in scale.

Stage 4

Stage 5

Weaving a trap

Many spiders trap their prey in webs. Each one begins with a single thread, which forms the basis for the intricate structure. Here (above) are the main stages of the web-weaving process.

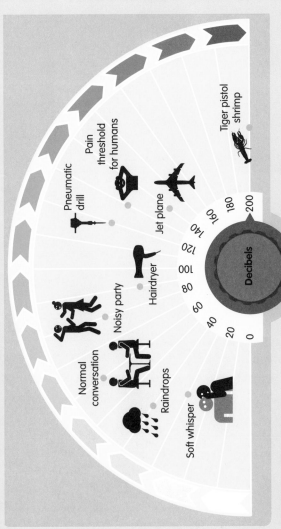

Noise nuisance

To stun its prey, the tiger pistol shrimp makes a short, snapping sound that is louder than a jet engine.

Sting in its tail

A fat-tailed scorpion emits venom from its tail to kill its victim. One sting containing just 0.5mg of fluid is toxic enough to kill 30 mice.

Minute creatures

There are more animals in your bed than in any zoo in the world. You don't notice them because they are so tiny. There are different types of minute creatures as well – they don't all live in your bed! Any animal between 0.5mm and 3mm in length is just about visible. Species smaller than this can only be seen under a microscope.

Swells up to 100 times its unfed volume

Hungry sheep tick

Full sheep tick

Not so tiny ticks
Bloodsucking ticks balloon in size while they feed.

Dust mite

Dust dwellers
One tablespoon-full, or 10g, of house dust contains up to 5,000 microscopic arachnids known as dust mites.

Tablespoon of house dust

5,000 dust mites

Dry and dormant

When their habitat dries up, some tiny creatures survive in an anhydrous state, which means they dry out and become dormant.

Brine shrimp

Sleeping chironomid

Extremely dry conditions
in which the animal becomes dormant

Bdelloid rotifer

Nematode

Radiation doses
1,000 times the strength needed to kill a human

Atmospheric pressure
6,000 times that of the pressure on Earth

What hazard?

In its anhydrous state, the microscopic, barrel-shaped tardigrade (or water bear) can survive in environmental conditions that would kill most other animals.

Boiling temperatures
of up to 151°C

Sub-zero temperatures
as low as -273°C

Animal champions

If animals had an Olympic team, they would probably come top in the medal table. The animals on these pages have evolved record-breaking adaptations to help them to survive in the wild. Some scientists study these animals so that they can mimic their special features in the design and engineering of materials and machines. Just imagine if there was a robot that could pull more than 1,141 times its own weight like the horned dung beetle can!

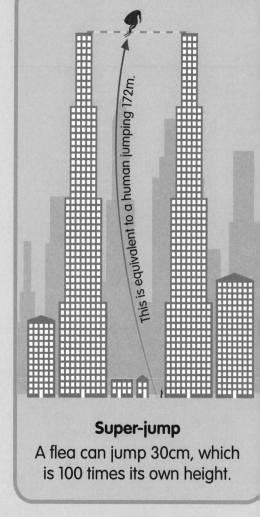

This is equivalent to a human jumping 172m.

Super-jump
A flea can jump 30cm, which is 100 times its own height.

The 200m dash
Peregrine falcons can cover 200m in less than half the time it takes the fastest land- and water-based animals.

Peregrine falcon	322km/h			
Cheetah	112.6km/h			
Sailfish	109.4km/h			
Pronghorn antelope	98.2km/h			
Ostrich	72.4km/h			
Greyhound	64.4km/h			
White rhino	56.3km/h			
Human man	38.6km/h			
Black spiny-tailed iguana	34.6km/h			
0m	20m	40m	60m	80m

Tug of weight
Horned dung beetles can pull the human equivalent of six double-decker buses.

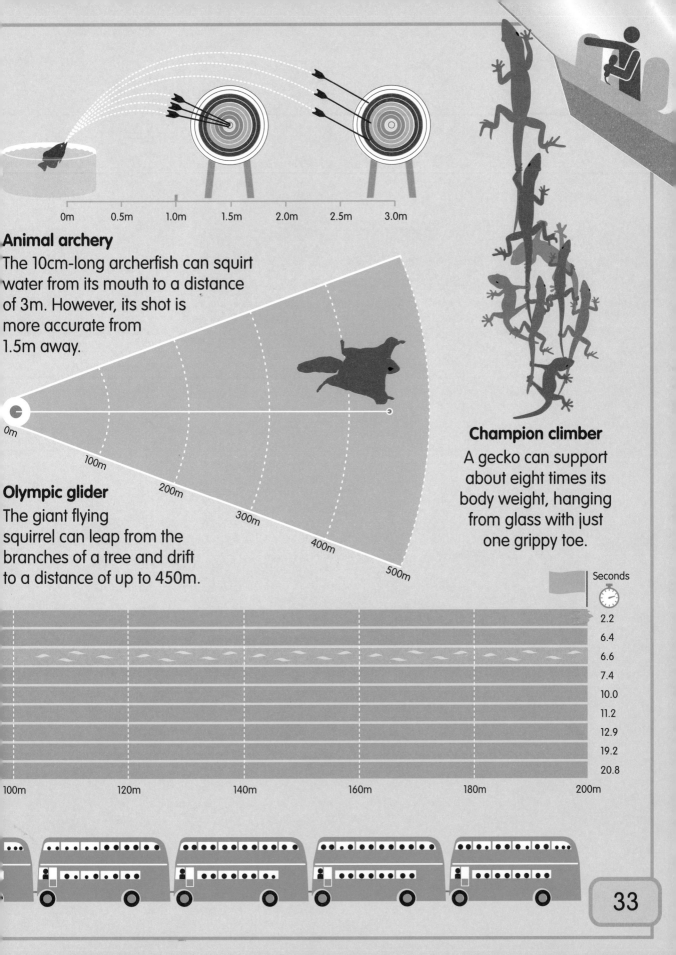

0m   0.5m   1.0m   1.5m   2.0m   2.5m   3.0m

Animal archery
The 10cm-long archerfish can squirt water from its mouth to a distance of 3m. However, its shot is more accurate from 1.5m away.

0m
100m
200m
300m
400m
500m

Champion climber
A gecko can support about eight times its body weight, hanging from glass with just one grippy toe.

Olympic glider
The giant flying squirrel can leap from the branches of a tree and drift to a distance of up to 450m.

Seconds

2.2
6.4
6.6
7.4
10.0
11.2
12.9
19.2
20.8

100m   120m   140m   160m   180m   200m

Animal senses

To find food, a mate or to avoid danger, animals rely on information gathered by their senses. The information is processed by the animal's nervous system, which tells the body how to respond. Many animals have senses that we don't have. For example, sharks can detect the electrical field created by the movement of their prey.

picnic area 30km

Smell
Sometimes life is a picnic for the silvertip grizzly bear – it can detect the smell of food up to 30km away.

Field of vision

Predators' eyes usually allow them to see forwards and downwards, where they might find prey. Prey tends to have good peripheral and upward vision (sight above and around them) because they can be attacked from above, behind or the side.

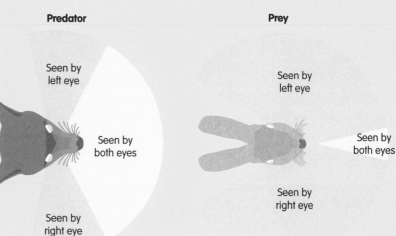

Predator

Seen by left eye

Seen by both eyes

Seen by right eye

Prey

Seen by left eye

Seen by both eyes

Seen by right eye

Animals that don't have eyes
5%

Animals with eyes
95%

Eye see you
Eyesight is important for most animals and nearly all animals can see.

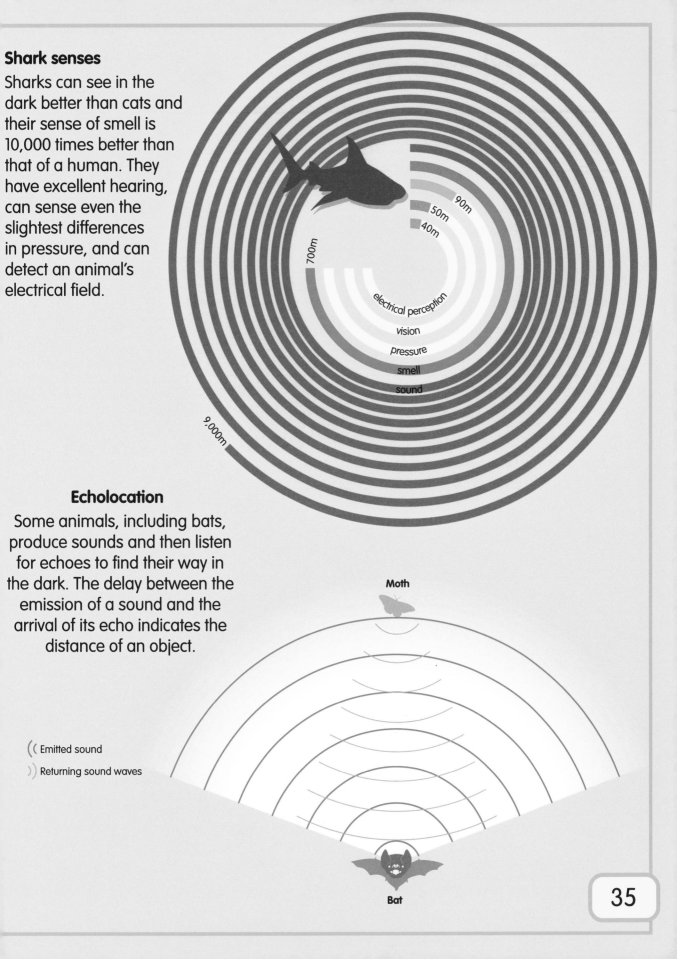

Shark senses

Sharks can see in the dark better than cats and their sense of smell is 10,000 times better than that of a human. They have excellent hearing, can sense even the slightest differences in pressure, and can detect an animal's electrical field.

90m

50m

40m

700m

electrical perception

vision

pressure

smell

sound

9,000m

Echolocation

Some animals, including bats, produce sounds and then listen for echoes to find their way in the dark. The delay between the emission of a sound and the arrival of its echo indicates the distance of an object.

Moth

((Emitted sound

)) Returning sound waves

Bat

35

Communication

Animals might not be able to speak, but they do communicate with each other. To transmit information, they send out signals using sounds, vibrations, displays of colour, scent or even dancing. The signals may be used to attract a mate, protect territory or warn other animals of danger.

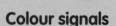

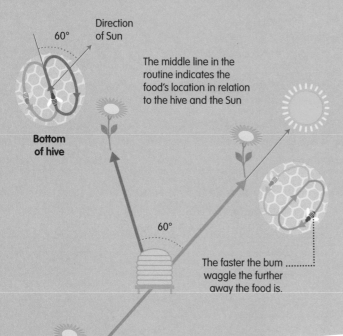

Direction of Sun

60°

The middle line in the routine indicates the food's location in relation to the hive and the Sun

Bottom of hive

60°

The faster the bum waggle the further away the food is.

Colour signals

A female panther chameleon changes her skin colouring to signal to males that she doesn't want to mate (left), or that she does (right).

Waggle dance

Scout bees waggle their bum and follow a figure-of-eight pattern in a dance routine that tells other bees where there is a good source of food.

Translation guide

Each of these body-language postures (right) explains how the dog is feeling.

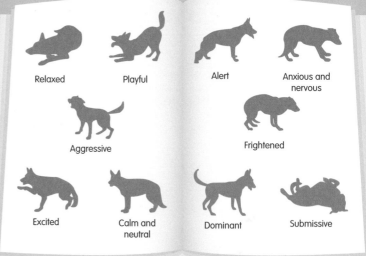

Relaxed

Playful

Alert

Anxious and nervous

Aggressive

Frightened

Excited

Calm and neutral

Dominant

Submissive

Communicating LOUDLY!

If all the animals in the world were the same size, the loudest one would be an insect called the lesser water boatman. Relative to their size, here are the volumes produced by other noisy animals.

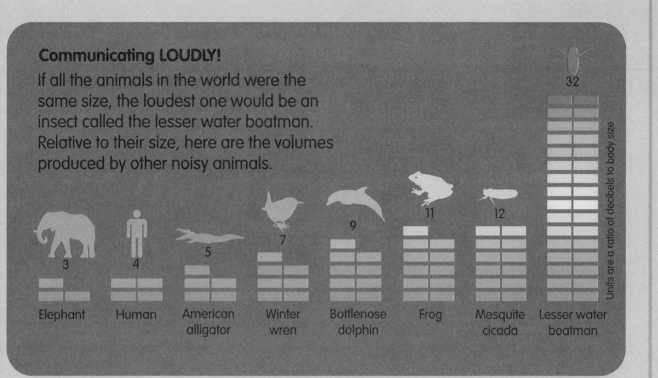

Units are a ratio of decibels to body size

Elephant	Human	American alligator	Winter wren	Bottlenose dolphin	Frog	Mesquite cicada	Lesser water boatman
3	4	5	7	9	11	12	32

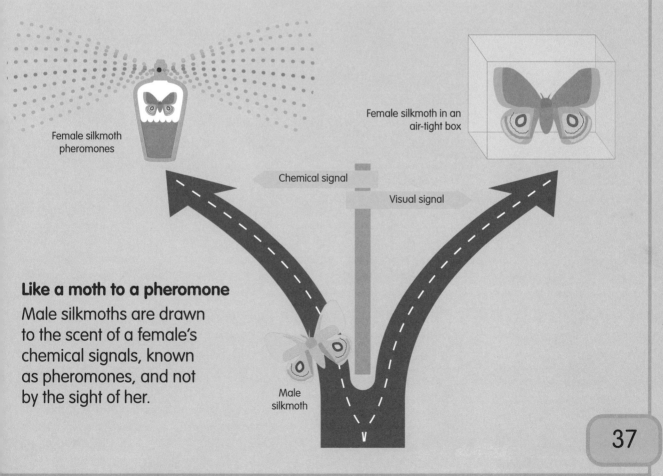

Female silkmoth pheromones

Female silkmoth in an air-tight box

Chemical signal

Visual signal

Like a moth to a pheromone

Male silkmoths are drawn to the scent of a female's chemical signals, known as pheromones, and not by the sight of her.

Male silkmoth

Hunters

Most meat-eating animals are equipped with specialist tools to help them capture and eat their prey. The hunting animals' weapons range from sharp teeth and claws to an ability to poison or shock their victims. There are animals that prefer to hunt alone and there are those that work together, often bringing down prey much larger than themselves.

Hunting party

Some hunters benefit from working in groups of the same species. The size of the hunting party depends on the type of animal in the group.

2 bald eagles

6 chimpanzees

12 bush dogs

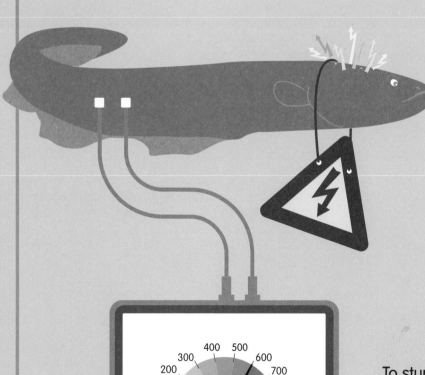

Volts

What a shocker!

To stun its prey or keep predators away, an electric eel generates a charge as powerful as two 240-volt electric sockets combined.

Gazelle hunters' scoreboard

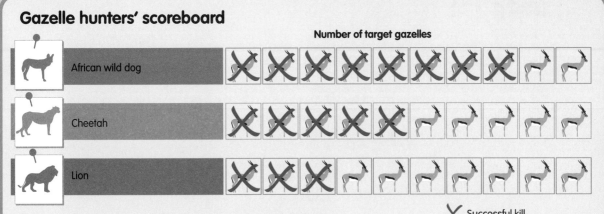

Number of target gazelles

African wild dog

Cheetah

Lion

X Successful kill

Some hunting species are more successful than others, even when they are hunting the same type of animal.

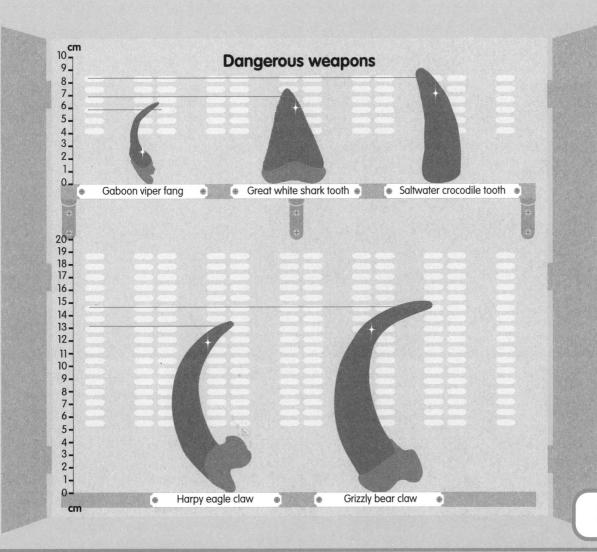

Dangerous weapons

Gaboon viper fang

Great white shark tooth

Saltwater crocodile tooth

Harpy eagle claw

Grizzly bear claw

Animal defences

To avoid being a predator's next meal, an animal may run away as fast as it can, play dead or hide. Other animals protect themselves in different ways. Some animals are covered in hard scales or spines that act like armour, and some warn off predators using poisons or stinky chemicals.

Opossum

05:59:00

Playing dead

Threatened opossums can play dead for up to six hours. During this time, the predator is put off by the prospect of eating old meat and so goes off to find a fresh meal elsewhere.

Running scared

Basilisk lizards have an extraordinary escape mechanism: they simply drop into the water and run across it. Here is how they do it.

Slap	Push	Lift

Each leg movement is made up of these three parts (top). The percentage (below) shows how much time is spent on each part of the movement.

13.9%	17.5%	68.6%

Human

Stink warning

The average person can detect the stinky smell emitted by a skunk up to 2.5km from the source.

2.5km ahead

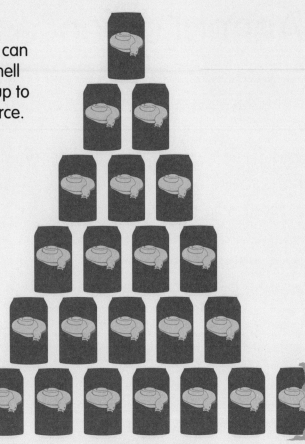

Slime soda

When it is bitten, a hagfish releases mucus from its body that makes its attacker choke. The slime produced in one minute would fill 22 drink cans.

Skipper catapulter

When it feels threatened, the skipper caterpillar shoots poo pellets at its enemy. These can travel up to 1.5m through the air, which is the human equivalent of 73m.

This green line is a scaled-down representation of the distance to which the caterpillar could fling its poo if the animal were human-sized.

 Human-sized caterpillar

Criminals

Some animals do things that would be considered crimes in the human world. For example, there are animals that steal food and there are those that injure or kill other animals, including humans. However, the perpetrators don't commit these 'crimes' out of greed, hatred or spite. They do so out of an instinct to survive.

Theft and vandalism
A locust can eat its own body weight in plant material in one day. Swarms of locusts devour every plant in their path.

Evidence

Suspect: Belcher's sea snake
Description of evidence: 6mg of venom
Victims: in theory, up to 1,000 human adults if the venom were delivered by some means other than a bite.

Possession of deadly venom
The Belcher's sea snake rarely bites. But, if it does, the venom it delivers is toxic enough to kill a person within 30 minutes.

Assault and public disorder
Up to 80 hyenas and one lion have been witnessed fighting over an animal carcass.

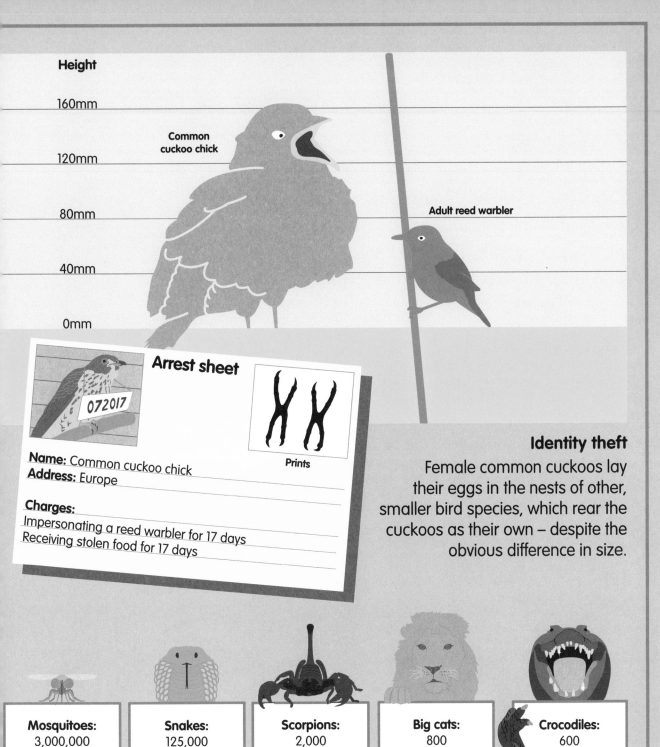

Height

160mm

Common cuckoo chick

120mm

Adult reed warbler

80mm

40mm

0mm

Arrest sheet

072017

Prints

Name: Common cuckoo chick
Address: Europe

Charges:
Impersonating a reed warbler for 17 days
Receiving stolen food for 17 days

Identity theft

Female common cuckoos lay their eggs in the nests of other, smaller bird species, which rear the cuckoos as their own – despite the obvious difference in size.

Mosquitoes: 3,000,000	Snakes: 125,000	Scorpions: 2,000	Big cats: 800	Crocodiles: 600

Rogues' gallery: human-killers

These shocking statistics reveal the number of people killed each year by the top five human-killers.

Courtship

Animals may not send flowers to their mates, but they still do all sorts of things to impress each other. Some of them are quite wacky, while others are rather romantic. Animals sing, dance, strut and sometimes even fight to impress a partner. They may even offer food or build a home for them.

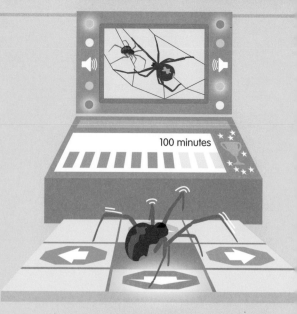

100 minutes

Dance and delight...or death

A male redback spider performs a 100 minute-long dance to impress a mate. If he stops too soon, the female spider kills him.

Funky gibbons

Every five days, male and female Siamang gibbon pairs sing a duet for 15 minutes to strengthen the bond between partners.

0   15 mins

Head-on collision

To win female partners, male American bighorn sheep charge at each other at speed and create spectacular crashes.

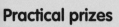

Practical prizes

The male in each of these bird species presents the female with a practical gift to prove to her that he would be a useful mating partner.

Fish for a fish

Common terns

Go nuts for nuts

Northern cardinals

Nab a nest

Blue-headed vireos

Growing up

Newborn animals are vulnerable to predators and the elements. Some animal mothers, or sometimes the fathers, look after their young until they grow big enough to fend for themselves. At a certain point in an animal's life, the creature becomes sexually mature and is able to produce its own young.

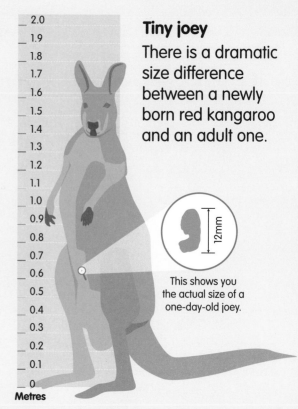

Tiny joey

There is a dramatic size difference between a newly born red kangaroo and an adult one.

12mm

This shows you the actual size of a one-day-old joey.

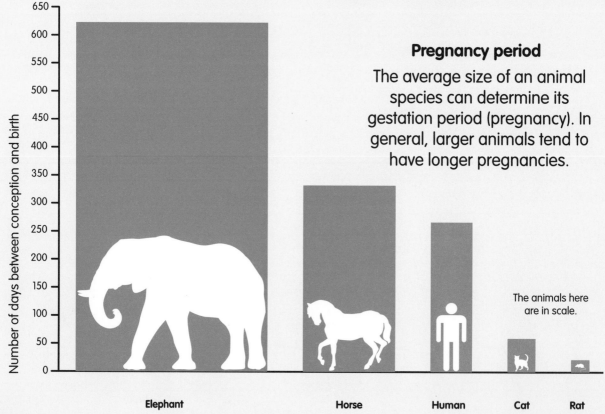

Pregnancy period

The average size of an animal species can determine its gestation period (pregnancy). In general, larger animals tend to have longer pregnancies.

The animals here are in scale.

Number of days between conception and birth

Elephant   Horse   Human   Cat   Rat

At what point in their lives do animals become sexually mature?

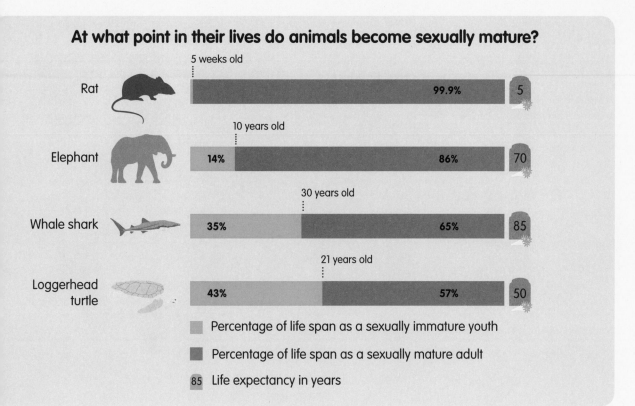

Rat — 5 weeks old — 99.9% — 5

Elephant — 10 years old — 14% — 86% — 70

Whale shark — 30 years old — 35% — 65% — 85

Loggerhead turtle — 21 years old — 43% — 57% — 50

Percentage of life span as a sexually immature youth

Percentage of life span as a sexually mature adult

85 Life expectancy in years

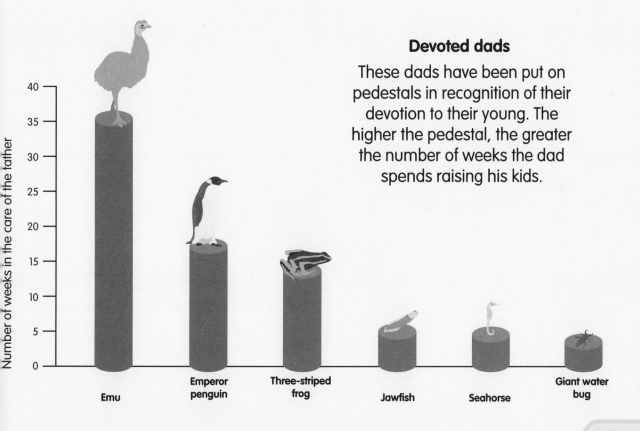

Devoted dads

These dads have been put on pedestals in recognition of their devotion to their young. The higher the pedestal, the greater the number of weeks the dad spends raising his kids.

Number of weeks in the care of the father

40
35
30
25
20
15
10
5
0

Emu   Emperor penguin   Three-striped frog   Jawfish   Seahorse   Giant water bug

Life expectancy

A Galápagos tortoise born on the same day as a human could live to see that person's great, great, great, great, great grandchild. One of the reasons why the reptile lives so long is because it burns energy slowly. As a general rule, highly active animals that burn energy quickly, such as those at the top of this chart, tend to have shorter life spans.

Expected life span

0 years
5
10
15
20
25
30
35
40
45

Bee
Mosquito fish
House mouse
Gerbil
Anole
Toucan
Newt
Hummingbird
Kangaroo
Rabbit
Domestic pigeon
Chipmunk
Civet
Chicken
Sea lion
Bullfrog
Leopard
Wolf
Beaver
Bottlenose dolphin
Dog
Tiger
Bat
Cat
Tiger salamander
Conger eel
Cobra
Bison
Tapir
Horse
Rhinoceros
Cockatiel
Grizzly bear
Canada goose
Deer
Lion
Toad
Chimpanzee

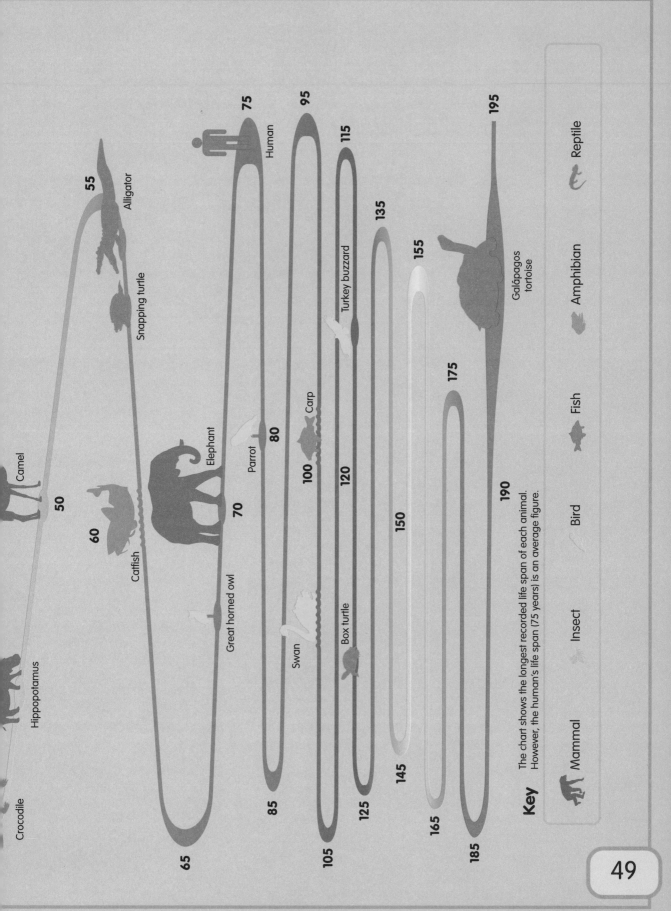

Crocodile

Hippopotamus

Camel

50

55 Alligator

Snapping turtle

60 Catfish

65

Elephant

Great horned owl

70

Parrot

75 Human

80

Swan

85

95

100 Carp

105

115

120

Box turtle

125

Turkey buzzard

135

145

150

155

165

175

185

190

195 Galápagos tortoise

Key The chart shows the longest recorded life span of each animal. However, the human's life span (75 years) is an average figure.

Mammal   Insect   Bird   Fish   Amphibian   Reptile

Animal homes

Animals make homes for a variety of reasons. They may need a place in which they can shelter from the elements or take refuge from predators. Some animals make homes in which to protect their young until they are able to fend for themselves. There are animals that spend a lot of time and effort building their homes, while others simply make use of natural features, such as caves or holes in trees.

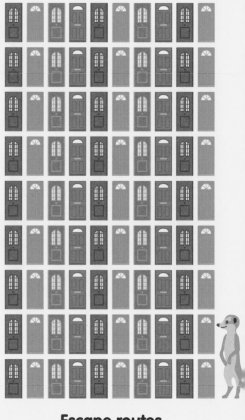

Escape routes

The burrows of meerkats have up to 90 different entrances into which the animals can scurry if a predator comes near.

45°C
113°F

65°C
149°F

Keeping cool

The top of flamingo nests in easter Africa are cooled by the breeze an can be up to 20°C colder than the surrounding ground.

Stone by stone

Horned coots build their mound nests in lakes using more than 3,000 stones. The stones are gathered one at a time by a mating pair.

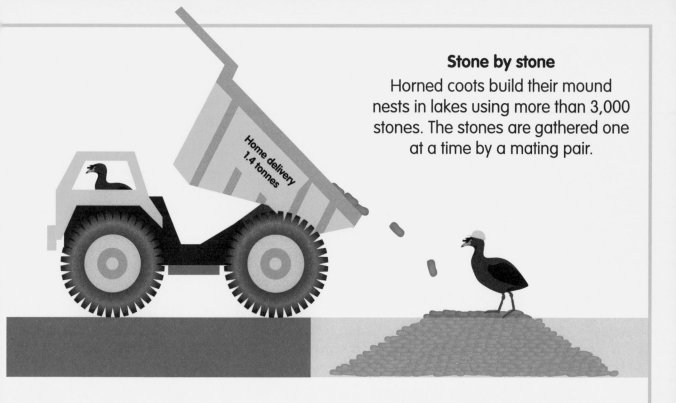

Home delivery 1.4 tonnes

Termite tower

If worker Macrotermes termites were human-sized, the nests they build would be up to 1.6km tall. The tallest human-built structure in the world is only half this height.

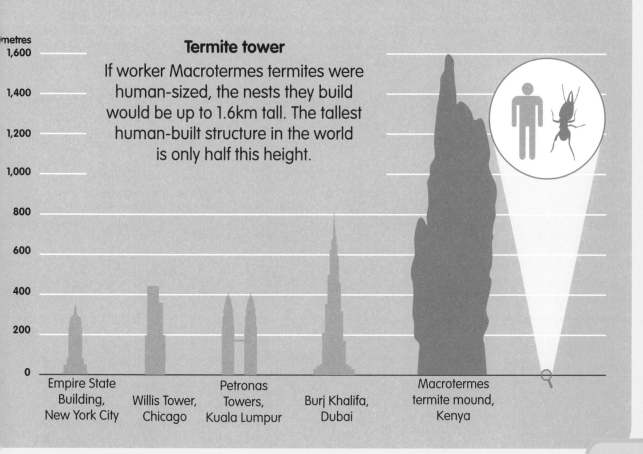

metres
1,600
1,400
1,200
1,000
800
600
400
200
0

Empire State Building, New York City

Willis Tower, Chicago

Petronas Towers, Kuala Lumpur

Burj Khalifa, Dubai

Macrotermes termite mound, Kenya

Migrating animals

Animals across the globe fly, swim, walk or drift in their effort to find food, a more pleasant climate or places to breed. These needs lead certain animals into difficult and often dangerous treks, some of which span thousands of kilometres. Some animals migrate each year between their summer and winter homes.

Zoom-in to the plains of eastern Africa to see the migration routes followed by herds of wildebeest.

Animal migration routes

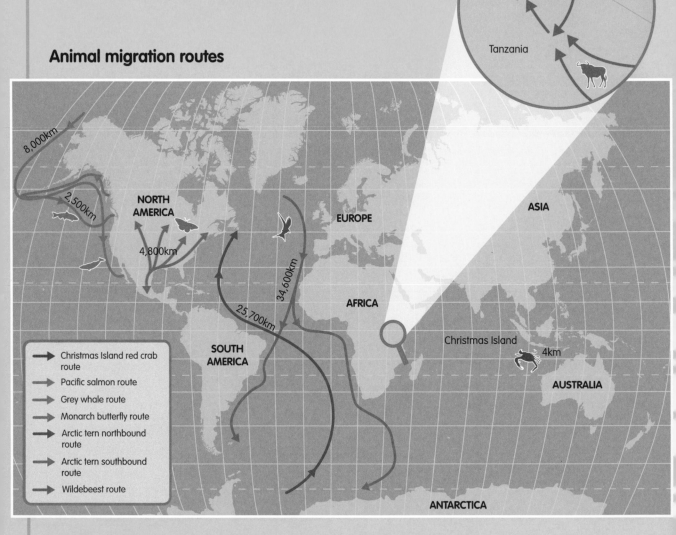

Kenya

1,800km

Tanzania

8,000km

2,500km

NORTH AMERICA

4,800km

34,600km

25,700km

NORTH AMERICA

EUROPE

ASIA

AFRICA

SOUTH AMERICA

Christmas Island

4km

AUSTRALIA

ANTARCTICA

Legend:
- Christmas Island red crab route
- Pacific salmon route
- Grey whale route
- Monarch butterfly route
- Arctic tern northbound route
- Arctic tern southbound route
- Wildebeest route

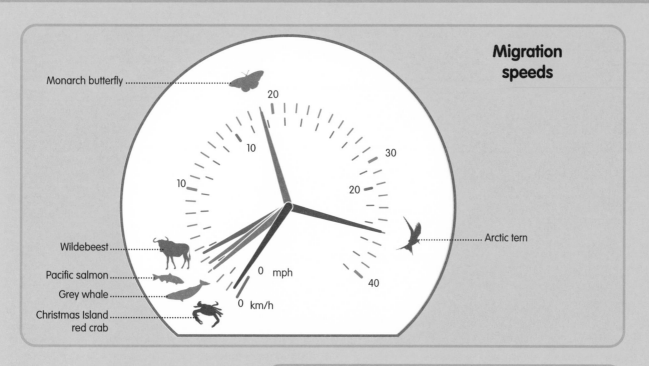

Migration speeds

Monarch butterfly ....

Wildebeest ....

Pacific salmon ....

Grey whale ....

Christmas Island ....
red crab

Arctic tern

20

10   30

10   20

0   mph

40

0   km/h

Out-of-this-world distance

An Arctic tern travels more than 2 million km in its lifetime. This is the equivalent of three round trips to the moon.

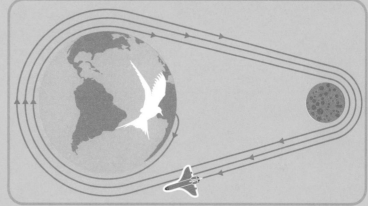

Ready for their annual trip

The number of days our featured animals spend travelling each year are represented here by suitcases and hand luggage.

180 days

105 days

92 days

67 days

37 days

7 days

Christmas Island   Monarch butterfly   Pacific salmon   Grey whale   Arctic tern   Wildebeest
red crab

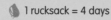 1 suitcase = 7 days   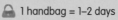 1 rucksack = 4 days   🔒 1 handbag = 1–2 days

Adaptations

All animals are adapted to survive in the habitats in which they live. Their adaptations are physical, or behavioural, or both. Over many generations, animal species gradually change and develop in response to their environment, in a process called evolution. The species we see today evolved from other animals that lived millions of years ago.

Natural anti-freeze

The Siberian salamander can survive in temperatures as low as -45°C, or even being frozen, by replacing water in its body with an anti-freeze chemical.

Animals in cold and rocky high altitudes

6,700m

5,000m

4,700m

4,000m

3,500m

Animal	Adaptations
Himalayan jumping spider	• Spins a silk sleeping bag to cope with extremely low temperatures
Himalayan marmot	• Thick fur • Hibernates in deep burrows
Golden snub-nosed monkey	• Thick fur • Can survive on mountain lichen and moss
Tibetan sand fox	• Thick fur
Mountain goat	• Rock-gripping hooves • Coat that traps warm air between two layers of hair
Tibetan spring snake	• Keeps warm in rivers and streams fed by hot springs
Mountain gorilla	• Long, dark hair that attracts the warmth of the sun

Heat-resistant

Before it goes out in the sun, the Saharan silver ant produces a protein that keeps its cells working in high temperatures.

Temperatures to hit 53°C today

When did today's animal groups first appear?

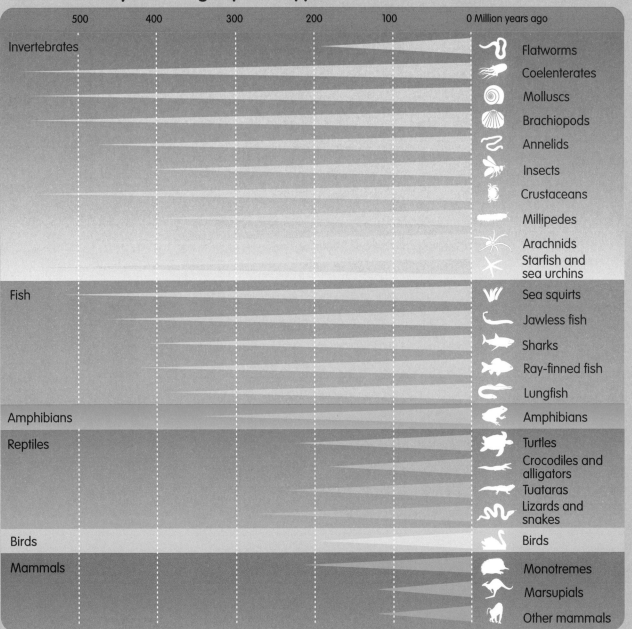

| 500 | 400 | 300 | 200 | 100 | 0 Million years ago |

Invertebrates
- Flatworms
- Coelenterates
- Molluscs
- Brachiopods
- Annelids
- Insects
- Crustaceans
- Millipedes
- Arachnids
- Starfish and sea urchins

Fish
- Sea squirts
- Jawless fish
- Sharks
- Ray-finned fish
- Lungfish

Amphibians
- Amphibians

Reptiles
- Turtles
- Crocodiles and alligators
- Tuataras
- Lizards and snakes

Birds
- Birds

Mammals
- Monotremes
- Marsupials
- Other mammals

Conservation

In the past 500 years, human activities have caused many animal species to become extinct (die out). Today, there is a long list of species that are under threat of extinction. Efforts are being made to protect them. This is done by controlling hunting, setting up nature reserves, or by reducing pollution or the destruction of habitats.

41%
Amphibian species

25%
Mammal species

13%
Bird species

5%
Reptile species

4%
Fish species

A selection of extinct species

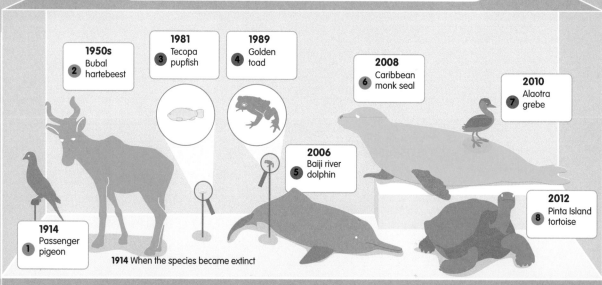

1950s
2 Bubal hartebeest

1981
3 Tecopa pupfish

1989
4 Golden toad

2008
6 Caribbean monk seal

2010
7 Alaotra grebe

2006
5 Baiji river dolphin

2012
8 Pinta Island tortoise

1914
1 Passenger pigeon

1914 When the species became extinct

Where did they live?

Key

● Hunted to extinction

● Lost its habitat

1 3 6 4 8 2 5 7

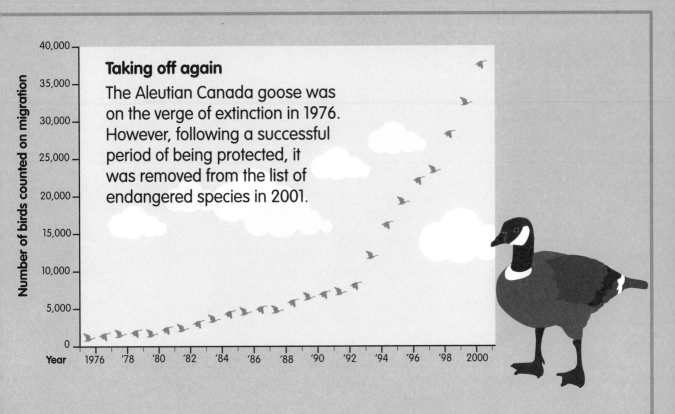

Taking off again

The Aleutian Canada goose was on the verge of extinction in 1976. However, following a successful period of being protected, it was removed from the list of endangered species in 2001.

Number of birds counted on migration (y-axis: 0 – 40,000)

Year (x-axis): 1976 '78 '80 '82 '84 '86 '88 '90 '92 '94 '96 '98 2000

Protected areas

Earth's land surface area is just one-third of the size of the ocean's surface area, yet much more land is protected.

- Protected ocean
- Protected land

3,922,518 sq km

22,297,050 sq km

1.17%

15%

Total ocean area
335,258,000 sq km

Total land area
148,647,000 sq km

Useful charts

Hummingbird

6,000 beats per minute

Chicken

275 beats per minute

How many times per minute does an animal's heart beat?

Pygmy shrew

1,300 beats per minute

Cheetah

120 beats per minute

More animal communication

Visual signals		
	1	Fireflies glow to attract mates.
	2	Cobras inflate their hood to scare off other animals.
	3	Cockatoos raise and lower their head crests to attract mates and to scare off other animals by making themselves look larger.
Sounds 	1	Elephants communicate with other elephants in far off herds by making sounds with their trunks.
	2	Wolves howl to call to other wolves in their pack.
	3	Male whales use whale song to communicate with female whales.
Touch 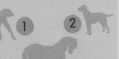	1	Chimpanzees groom each other to strengthen the bond between them.
	2	Dogs lick their pups to bond with them, as well as to clean them.
	3	Horses kick other horses to establish who is the dominant (more powerful) one.
Chemicals 	1	Ants leave chemical trails so that other ants know which way they went.
	2	Black bears communicate with each other by marking objects, such as trees, with their scent.
	3	Skunks warn off predators by giving off a smelly chemical.

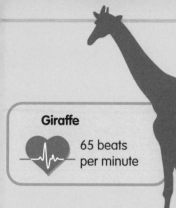

Giraffe
♥ 65 beats per minute

Elephant
♥ 30 beats per minute

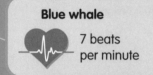

Blue whale
♥ 7 beats per minute

Footprints and tracks

Animal	Animal shape	Footprints	Tracks
Weasel			
Turkey			
Fox			
Tiger			
Dog			
Deer			
Crow			

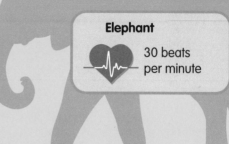

59

Glossary

adaptation
A special feature of a living thing that makes it better suited to its particular environment or way of life.

arachnid
An invertebrate with four pairs of legs.

arthropod
An invertebrate animal with jointed legs, a segmented body and exoskeleton.

brooding
When adult animals use their body to keep their eggs or young warm.

burrow
A hole or tunnel dug into the ground by an animal to create a home or a refuge from predators.

cartilage
A tough, flexible tissue found on the skeleton of vertebrates. The skeletons of sharks and rays are made entirely of cartilage.

courtship
The displays and behaviours that animals use to attract a mate.

crustacean
A group of arthropods that includes crabs and shrimps.

dormant
During a dormant period an animal's normal physical functions slow down or stop working.

evolution
The process by which different kinds of living organisms developed and diversified from earlier, often less complex life forms during the history of Earth.

exoskeleton
An external skeleton that supports and protects an animal's body. A crab's tough shell is its exoskeleton.

extinction
The permanent disappearance of a species.

gestation period
The period of development of an animal from the time it is conceived until its birth.

hibernation
When an animal spends the cold winter in a dormant state.

incubate
To hatch eggs by sitting on them and keeping them warm.

insect
A small arthropod with six legs and three body parts: head, thorax and abdomen. Insects generally have two or four wings.

invertebrate
An animal without a backbone. About 95 per cent of all animals are invertebrates.

life cycle
The pattern of changes that occur to an animal as it develops over its lifetime.

life expectancy
The average period of time an animal is expected to live.

marsupial
A mammal that develops inside its mother's pouch when it is a newborn.

mating
The coming together of a male and female animal during sexual reproduction.

moult
When an animal sheds its outer covering. Insects and crustaceans have to moult so that they can grow bigger.

parasite
A living thing that lives on or inside the body of another species of living thing, known as a host.

pheromone
A chemical emitted by an animal that has an effect on another of the same species.

predator
An animal that kills and eats other animals.

prey
An animal that is hunted and killed by another animal for food.

regeneration
The re-growth of a body part, such as a leg or a tail.

reproduction
The production of offspring (young animals).

scales
Hard, overlapping plates that protect the skin of fish and reptiles.

species
A group of living organisms that contains individuals that can breed with each other.

streamlined
Describes an animal's body that is shaped to move through water or air easily.

venom
A poisonous fluid in an animal's bite or sting. Poison, by contrast, is swallowed or inhaled by the victim.

vertebrate
An animal with a backbone. There are five main types of vertebrates: mammals, birds, fish, reptiles and amphibians.

Index

A

adaptations 54–55, 60
albatrosses 15
alligators 17, 37, 48, 55
American bighorn sheep 45
amphibians 9, 18–19, 49, 55, 56
anhydrous state 31
anti-freeze chemicals 54
ants 55, 58
arachnids 26, 27, 29, 30, 55, 60
Arctic terns 52, 53
arthropods 26

B

bats 10, 12, 35, 48
bears 10, 39, 48, 58
bees 36, 48
beetles, horned dung 32
bioluminescent light 24
birds 9, 14–15, 43, 45, 49, 55, 56, 57
blood, squirting 17
blood-suckers 28, 30
body language 36
bones 9, 16, 20
breathing 18, 20
butterflies, monarch 52, 53

C

caecilians 19
camels 11, 13, 48
caterpillars 40, 41
cartilage 20, 60
cats 8, 10, 43, 46, 48
chameleons 36
cheetahs 32, 39, 58
chimpanzees 12, 38, 48, 58
claws 39
coelacanths 20
communication 36–37, 58
conservation 56–57
cows 12, 13
crabs 28, 52, 53
crocodiles 8, 16, 17, 39, 43, 48, 55
crustaceans 26, 28, 29, 55, 60

D

deer 59
defences 17, 18, 24, 40–41
diving 15
dogs 8, 10, 32, 36, 38, 39, 48, 58, 59
dolphins 37, 48
ducks 14, 57
dust mites 30

E

eagles 38, 39
echidnas 10
echolocation 35
eels 20, 25, 38, 48
eggs 10, 14, 15, 16, 17, 18, 20
electricity 35, 38
elephants 10, 13, 37, 46, 47, 49, 58, 59

emus 47
evolution 54, 60
extinction 56, 60
eyes 24, 27, 34

F

fish 9, 20–25, 32, 33, 41, 45, 47, 49, 55, 56
flamingos 50
fleas 32
flying 14, 32
food 11, 12, 13, 24, 28
foxes 8, 54, 59
frogs 18, 19, 37, 47
fur 10, 11, 54

G

gibbons 44
giraffes 12, 59
gliding 15, 33
gorillas 54
growing 21, 46–47
guinea pigs 11

H

hair 10, 11, 54
hibernation 12
horses 11, 46, 48, 58
humans 10, 12, 13, 15, 32, 37, 43, 46, 49
hummingbirds 14, 48, 58
hunting 13, 24, 38–39
hyenas 42

IJ

insects 26, 27, 37, 49, 55, 60
invertebrates 9, 26–29, 55, 61

KL

kangaroos 8, 10, 46, 48
koalas 12
lions 10, 13, 39, 42, 48
lizards 17, 40
locusts 42

M

mammals 8, 9, 10–13, 49, 55, 56
marmots 12, 54
marsupials 55, 61
mating 18, 44–45, 61
meat-eaters 8, 28–29, 38–39
meerkats 50
mice 10, 12, 29, 48
migration 52–53
milk 10, 11
monkeys 10, 54
mosquitoes 43
moths 37
moulting 26, 27, 61
mountain goats 54
musk oxen 11

NO

nests 45, 50, 51
oceans 9, 15, 20, 24–25, 57
opossums 40
ostriches 14, 15, 32
otters, sea 11

PQ

parasites 28, 30, 61
penguins 14, 15, 47
peregrine falcons 32
pheromones 37, 61
pigs 13
platypuses 10
predators 8, 28–29, 34, 38–39, 61

R

rats 10, 46, 47
regeneration 18
reptiles 9, 16–17, 48, 49, 55, 56

S

salamanders 19, 48, 54
salmon, Pacific 52, 53
scales 21, 40, 61
scorpions 29, 43
seals 10, 11, 12
sharks 20, 21, 24, 34, 35, 39, 47, 55
shrews 10, 13, 58
shrimps 29, 31
skunks 41, 58
sleep 12, 13
smell 35, 37, 41
snakes 16, 17, 39, 42, 43, 54
species 8, 10, 17, 20, 26, 56, 61
spiders 27, 29, 54, 44
squid 24, 26

squirrels, giant gliding 33
survival 12, 31, 32, 40–43, 54
swimming 22–23

TU

tardigrades 31
teeth 39
temperature, body 10, 12, 16, 18, 54, 55
termites 51
terrapins 17
ticks 30
tigers 59
tortoises 17, 48, 49
turtles 17, 47, 48, 49, 55

V

venom 29, 42, 61
vertebrates 9, 61

WXYZ

waste 13
webs 29
whales 10, 13, 52, 53, 58, 59
wildebeest 52, 53
wings 14, 15, 27
wolves 8, 48, 58
worms 26, 28, 55
young 10, 11, 16, 17, 18, 19, 46–47

Find out more

 **Books to read**

Everything You Need to Know about Animals by Nicola Davies (Kingfisher, 2013)
Navigators: Animals by Miranda Smith (Kingfisher, 2012)
Encyclopedia of Animals by Karen McGhee and George McKay, Ph.D (National Geographic, 2009)
Usborne World of Animals by Susanna Davidson and Mike Unwin (Usborne, 2006)
DK Eyewitness Animals by DK Publishing (Dorling Kindersley, 2012)

 Websites to visit

A website that catalogues animals from aardvarks to zebras:
http://animals.nationalgeographic.com/animals

Marvel at Australian marsupials:
www.australianwildlife.com.au/marsupials.htm

See animals pretending to be a different species, and discover why:
www.bbc.co.uk/nature/adaptations/Mimicry

Find out more about animals that develop in their mother's pouch:
www.sandiegozoo.org/animalbytes/t-marsupial.html

🏛 **Places to visit**

Meet different types of mammals in the Blue Zone at:
The Natural History Museum, Cromwell Road, London SW7 5BD, UK
Telephone: +44 (0) 20 7942 5000
www.nhm.ac.uk

Dive into the world of aquatic animals at:
The Blue Reef Aquarium, Towan Promenade, Newquay, Cornwall, TR7 1DU, UK
Telephone: +44 (0)1637 878 134
www.bluereefaquarium.co.uk/newquay/

Twitching to learn more about wild birds? Take a flying visit to:
Wildfowl & Wetlands Trust, Slimbridge, Gloucestershire, GL2 7BT, UK
Telephone: +44 (0)1453 891 900
www.wwt.org.uk